THE BEST
**DOGS**
EVER

# COCKER SPANIELS ARE THE BEST!

## Elaine Landau

⌐ LERNER PUBLICATIONS COMPANY · MINNEAPOLIS

**To Diane R. Chen**

Lerner Publications Company
A division of Lerner Publishing Group, Inc.
241 First Avenue North
Minneapolis, MN 55401 U.S.A.

Website address: www.lernerbooks.com

Library of Congress Cataloging-in-Publication Data

Landau, Elaine.
      Cocker spaniels are the best! / by Elaine Landau.
         p.   cm. — (The best dogs ever)
      Includes index.
      ISBN 978-0-7613-5056-9 (lib. bdg. : alk. paper)
      1. Cocker spaniels—Juvenile literature.  I. Title.
      SF429.C55L35  2011
      636.752'4—dc22                        2009037560

Manufactured in the United States of America
1 — BP — 7/15/10

# TABLE OF CONTENTS

**CHAPTER ONE**
## THE VERY MERRY COCKER SPANIEL
### 4

**CHAPTER TWO**
## WAY BACK WHEN
### 11

**CHAPTER THREE**
## THE RIGHT DOG FOR YOU?
### 18

**CHAPTER FOUR**
## WELCOME HOME
### 24

Glossary . . . . 30    For More Information . . . . 31    Index . . . . 32

# CHAPTER ONE
# THE VERY MERRY COCKER SPANIEL

Would a happy dog with long, floppy ears appeal to you? What if this dog was smart and loyal too? This pooch's pluses don't stop here either. It's also loving and playful.

Did you guess that this dog is a **cocker spaniel?** People call them cockers for short. These dogs have brains, beauty, and loads of canine charm. Cockers have stolen the hearts of humans for years.

# Sturdy and Proud

The cocker is a sturdy, medium-sized dog. Males stand about 15 inches (38 centimeters) high at the shoulder. Females are about 1 inch (3 cm) shorter. These dogs weigh from 15 to 30 pounds (7 to 14 kilograms). That's about as much as three house cats.

A cocker spaniel's size makes it a perfect house pet. Cockers are neither too big nor too small.

## Quite a Coat

Cockers are great-looking dogs from head to toe. They are known for their silky coats and long ears. Their fur may be either straight or wavy.

These dogs come in lots of colors too. They can be cream, black, red, tan, or brown. Other cockers are more than one color. Black and white and red and white are common combinations.

## A STAR ON THE BIG SCREEN

Have you ever seen the movie *Lady and the Tramp*? The two dogs in the movie have quite an adventure. The classy canine star, Lady, is a cocker!

## A Joy to Be With

Cockers are sweet, cheerful, and active. These alert dogs learn quickly. And they are easy to train. They want to please their owners.

These smart dogs love to learn new tricks.

Cockers love being around people. Some folks say that these dogs sense their owners' moods. Cockers try to be part of the family. They get along well with children and other pets. Their owners think cocker spaniels are the best!

# NOTHING BUT THE BEST!

You'll need a great name for your super dog. The name you pick should fit your pooch perfectly. Are any of these a good match?

Lady

SASSY

Jazz

ENZO

Dusty

Maggie

BANDIT

Buffy

TAFFY

Curly

# CHAPTER TWO
# WAY BACK WHEN

The cocker spaniel is one of the oldest dog breeds. It got its start in Spain. There, it was used as a hunting dog.

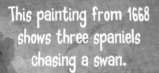

This painting from 1668 shows three spaniels chasing a swan.

This British painting from 1771 shows a hunting spaniel following a scent.

Cocker spaniels were good trackers. They easily picked up the scent of birds and other prey. They were hardworking dogs that seemed to enjoy their job.

Francisco Goya, a famous Spanish artist, painted this picture of King Charles IV of Spain and his spaniel in the late 1700s.

## Moving On

In time, people brought these dogs to Britain. They hunted there too. In the late 1870s, cockers arrived in the United States. Some cockers were used for hunting. Others became much-loved pets.

In 1792, an artist painted the princesses Mary, Sophia, and Amelia of Great Britain playing with pet spaniels.

British artist Richard Ansdell painted this hunting spaniel in the late 1800s.

By the close of the 1800s, cockers often appeared in dog shows. Judges seemed to like these pretty pooches. Cockers took home more than their share of medals and ribbons.

A prizewinning cocker (left) meets another dog at a 1910 dog show in Great Britain.

# A BUNCH OF BEAUTIES!

Cockers are real winners. These super dogs have won Best in Show at the Westminster Kennel Club Dog Show four times!

In 1921, a dog named Midkiff's Seductive took the title. Then, in 1940, the title went to a champ called My Own Brucie (right). Brucie became quite famous. He won Best in Show again the next year. In 1954, still another cocker won. This time, the honor went to Camor's Rise and Shine.

By the 1930s, cockers were in great demand. Many families wanted to own one. These great dogs are still popular.

A cocker joins a father and son for a hunting trip in Minnesota, about 1930.

A woman prepares her cocker for a dog show in 1955.

# A Sporting Dog

The American Kennel Club (AKC) groups different dogs by breed. Breeds that have some things in common are grouped together. Some AKC groups are the working group, the hound group, and the toy group.

The komondor is part of the working group.

The beagle is part of the hound group.

The Yorkshire terrier is part of the toy group.

# A DIFFERENT KIND OF WORK

Some cockers are trained as therapy dogs. These dogs visit hospitals and nursing homes. They cheer up the patients there. Cockers enjoy being around people. They are perfect for this job.

The cocker spaniel is in the sporting group. It is the smallest dog in this group. All sporting group dogs are good hunters. The cocker spaniel fits in well.

Sporting dogs chase and retrieve animals for hunters. This cocker spaniel fetched a duck its owner shot.

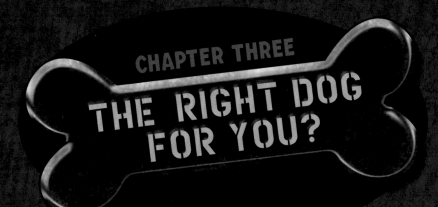

# CHAPTER THREE

# THE RIGHT DOG FOR YOU?

Cockers are hard to pass up. Who wouldn't want a beautiful dog that's also fun? But that doesn't mean you should get one. The dog you pick should be a good match for you and your family. Read on to see if a cocker fits the bill.

## A Dog That Needs People

Your cocker will want to spend lots of time with you. It will follow you from room to room. Cockers are not loners. These dogs need to be with people. Some howl when left alone for too long. Would you want a dog like this, or would it annoy you? And what about your neighbors?

## FROM BLUE TO BROWN

Could you fall in love with a cocker's big, brown eyes? Not at first. Most of these dogs are born with blue eyes. Their eye color slowly changes during their first year of life.

# Gosh, This Dog Needs Grooming!

Cockers have beautiful coats. But it takes lots of grooming for them to look their best. Their coats need to be brushed and clipped. Many cocker owners take their dogs to groomers. But this can be costly. Be sure your family can afford the grooming bills.

A groomer will trim your cocker's nails too.

## An Active Canine

Are you a couch potato? Is your idea of exercise going to the kitchen for a snack? If so, don't get a cocker. Cockers are active dogs that love to play. They enjoy long walks and Frisbee games.

# City Pooch/ Country Pooch

Cockers do well in both the city and the country. They are not too big to live in city apartments. If you live in a city, try to find a grassy place to walk your dog in the summer. Concrete can burn a cocker's paws on hot days.

## DOGS OF THE RICH AND FAMOUS

No one can deny a cocker's appeal. Business person and entertainer Oprah Winfrey (left) and actor William Baldwin have owned cockers. A few U.S. presidents have also had these darling dogs. Ronald Reagan and Harry S. Truman both had cockers.

## A Good Choice

Is a cocker the right dog for you? If so, you're lucky. The newest member of your family will be fine looking, friendly, and lots of fun!

# CHAPTER FOUR

# WELCOME HOME

The day you've been waiting for is finally here.
Love on four feet is coming to your house to stay.
You're getting your very own cocker spaniel.

It's an exciting time. But with all the joy and excitement you feel, don't forget your dog's needs. Plan to spend much of the day with your new pet. Make your dog feel safe and comfortable in its new home.

This cocker puppy is twelve weeks old. That's old enough to leave its mother and come to a new home.

# Be Ready

Get off to a smooth start. Get the supplies you'll need ahead of time. Here's a useful list of doggy basics:

- collar

- leash

- tags (for identification)

- dog food

- food and water bowls

- crates (one for when your pet travels and one for it to rest in at home)

- treats (to be used in training)

- toys

Get food and water bowls with tall sides for your cocker. That will keep your dog's floppy ears from getting in the way.

# Find a Good Vet

Take your dog to a veterinarian right away. That's a doctor who treats animals. They are called vets for short.

Your vet will help you keep your dog healthy. Your dog should see a vet for checkups and to get the shots it needs. And be sure to bring your dog to the vet if it gets sick.

## A HEALTHFUL DIET

Ask your vet what to feed your dog. Dogs need different food at different stages of their lives. Don't give your dog table scraps. This can lead to an unhealthful weight gain.

Don't leave food lying around the house. Your cocker will help itself to groceries or garbage.

# Good Grooming

Grooming a cocker takes work. You'll need to brush your dog every day. You must also keep your dog clean. Some people keep their dog's coat short. That makes grooming easier.

A dog comb helps keep your dog's fur tangle-free.

# Your New Best Friend

Cockers are great to have around. Make your dog feel like part of the family. Take it on family picnics. Cockers enjoy trips to a lake or a park too. Let your dog meet and greet your guests as well. Cockers like people, and people like them.

Give your dog all the love and care it needs. Your cocker will repay you every day in many different ways. You'll have a wonderful best friend for years to come.

## YEARS OF LOVE

With good food and care, a cocker can live from twelve to fifteen years.

# GLOSSARY

**American Kennel Club (AKC):** an organization that groups dogs by breed. The AKC also defines the characteristics of different breeds.

**breed:** a particular type of dog. Dogs of the same breed have the same body shape and general features.

**canine:** a dog, or having to do with dogs

**coat:** a dog's fur

**groom:** to clean, brush, and trim a dog's coat

**prey:** an animal that is hunted for food

**sporting group:** a group of dogs that tend to be active and alert. Dogs in the sporting group make good hunters.

**therapy dog:** a dog brought to nursing homes or hospitals to comfort patients

**veterinarian:** a doctor who treats animals. Veterinarians are called vets for short.

# FOR MORE INFORMATION

## Books

Brecke, Nicole, and Patricia M. Stockland. *Dogs You Can Draw.* Minneapolis: Millbrook Press, 2010. Perfect for dog lovers, this colorful book teaches readers how to draw many different popular dog breeds.

Gray, Susan H. *Cocker Spaniels.* Mankato, MN: Child's World, 2008. Readers will find a close-up look at cocker spaniels in this book.

Landau, Elaine. *Your Pet Dog.* Rev. ed. New York: Children's Press, 2007. This is a good guide for young people on choosing and caring for a dog.

MacAulay, Kelley, and Bobbie Kalman. *Cocker Spaniels.* New York: Crabtree, 2007. This book offers some good information on grooming, feeding, and exercising cocker spaniels.

## Websites

### American Kennel Club
http://www.akc.org
Visit this site to find a complete listing of AKC-registered dog breeds, including the cocker spaniel. This site also features fun printable activities for kids.

### American Spaniel Club: Owning a Cocker
http://www.asc-cockerspaniel.org/index.php/owning-a-cocker.html
Learn whether a cocker spaniel is the right breed for your family.

### ASPCA Animaland
http://www2.aspca.org/site/PageServer?pagename=kids_pc_home
Check out this page for helpful hints on caring for a dog and other pets.

# Index

American Kennel Club
  (AKC), 16

coat, 7, 20
color, 8

exercise, 21

food, 26-27

grooming, 20, 28

health, 27

history, 11-15
hunting, 11-13, 17

names, 10

size, 6
sporting group, 17

therapy dogs, 17

Westmister Kennel Club
  Dog Show, 14

# Photo Acknowledgments

The images in this book are used with the permission of: backgrounds © iStockphoto.com/Julie Fisher and © iStockphoto.com/Tomasz Adamczyk; © iStockphoto.com/Michael Balderas, p. 1; © Dave King/Dorling Kindersley/Getty Images, p. 4; © iStockphoto.com/Eric Isselée, pp. 4-5, 8-9; © Michelangelo Gratton/Digital Vision/Getty Images, p. 5; © Juniors Bildarchiv/Alamy, pp. 6-7, 8 (top), 26 (bottom); © iStockphoto.com/Konstantin Grebnev, p. 7 (top); © Sergey Lavrentev/Dreamstime.com, p. 7 (bottom); © Walt Disney Pictures/Courtesy Everett Collection, p. 9 (top); © van hilversum/Alamy, p. 9 (bottom); © Plush Studios/Digital Vision/Getty Images, p. 10 (top); © Eriklam/Dreamstime.com, p. 10 (bottom); © Abraham Danielsz. Hondius/The Bridgeman Art Library/Getty Images, p. 11; © George Stubbs/The Bridgeman Art Library/Getty Images, p. 12 (top); The Art Archive/Museo di Capodimonte, Naples/Gianni Dagli Orti, p. 12 (bottom); © The Bridgeman Art Library/Getty Images, p. 13 (top); © Guildhall Art Gallery/HIP/Art Resource, NY, p. 13 (bottom); © W.G. Phillips/Hulton Archive/Getty Images, p. 14 (top); © Underwood & Underwood/CORBIS, p. 14 (bottom); © Minnesota Historical Society/CORBIS, p. 15 (top); © Three Lions/Hulton Archive/Getty Images, p. 15 (bottom); © Eric Isselée/Dreamstime.com, p. 16 (left); © Tracy Morgan/Dorling Kindersley/Getty Images, pp. 16 (top right), 27 (bottom); © Erik Lam/Shutterstock Images, p. 16 (bottom right); © Dep/Marin Independent Journal/ZUMA Press, p. 17 (top); © tbkmedia.de/Alamy, p. 17 (bottom); © RF Company/Alamy, p. 18; © age fotostock/SuperStock, pp. 19 (top), 25 (bottom); © Mario Mage/Photolibrary/Getty Images, p. 19 (bottom); © TongRo Image Stock/Alamy, p. 20 (top); © Choice/Alamy, p. 20 (bottom); © Alex Mares-Manton/Asia Images/Getty Images, p. 21; © iStockphoto.com/Jan Rihak, p. 22; © Poutnik/Dreamstime.com, pp. 22-23; © Kevin Winter/ImageDirect/Getty Images, p. 23 (top); © Andrew Linscott/Alamy, p. 24; © Jupiterimages/Comstock/Getty Images, p. 25 (top); © Tammy Mcallister/Dreamstime.com, p. 26 (top); © April Turner/Dreamstime.com, p. 26 (second from top); © iStockphoto.com/orix3, p. 26 (second from bottom); © Tom Grill/CORBIS, p. 27 (top); AP Photo/Chris Gardner, p. 28 (top); © Dorling Kindersley/Getty Images, p. 28 (bottom); © iStockphoto.com/Duncan Walker, p. 29.

Front and Back Cover: © Eric Isselée/Dreamstime.com.